To Margie —
We swear we don't laugh
at Chatchka when she
misses the couch. Snicker
may be. A mild snort perhaps.
But we show respect —
Merry Xmas — 1987
the dog's adoptive folks.

NEVER TAKE YOUR CAT TO A SALAD BAR

NEW SYLVIA CARTOONS BY

Nicole Hollander

Vintage Books
A Division of Random House
New York

A Vintage Original, December 1987
First Edition
Copyright ©1987 by Nicole Hollander

Library of Congress Cataloging-in-Publication Data
Hollander, Nicole.
   Never take your cat to a salad bar.
   "A Vintage original"—Verso t.p.
   1. American wit and humor, Pictorial.   I. Title.
II. Title: Sylvia.
NC1429.H588A4 1987   741.5'973   87-40100
ISBN 0-394-75558-8 (pbk.)

Design by Tom Greensfelder + Steve Strong
Manufactured in the United States of America
10 9 8 7 6 5 4 3 2 1

Superwoman / Travel Agent / Therapist

You're depressed. You feel old, which is nonsense, but anyway I made reservations. You'll take the Concorde to Paris on Tuesday.

Yes. Uh-huh. How did you know? Who the heck are you?

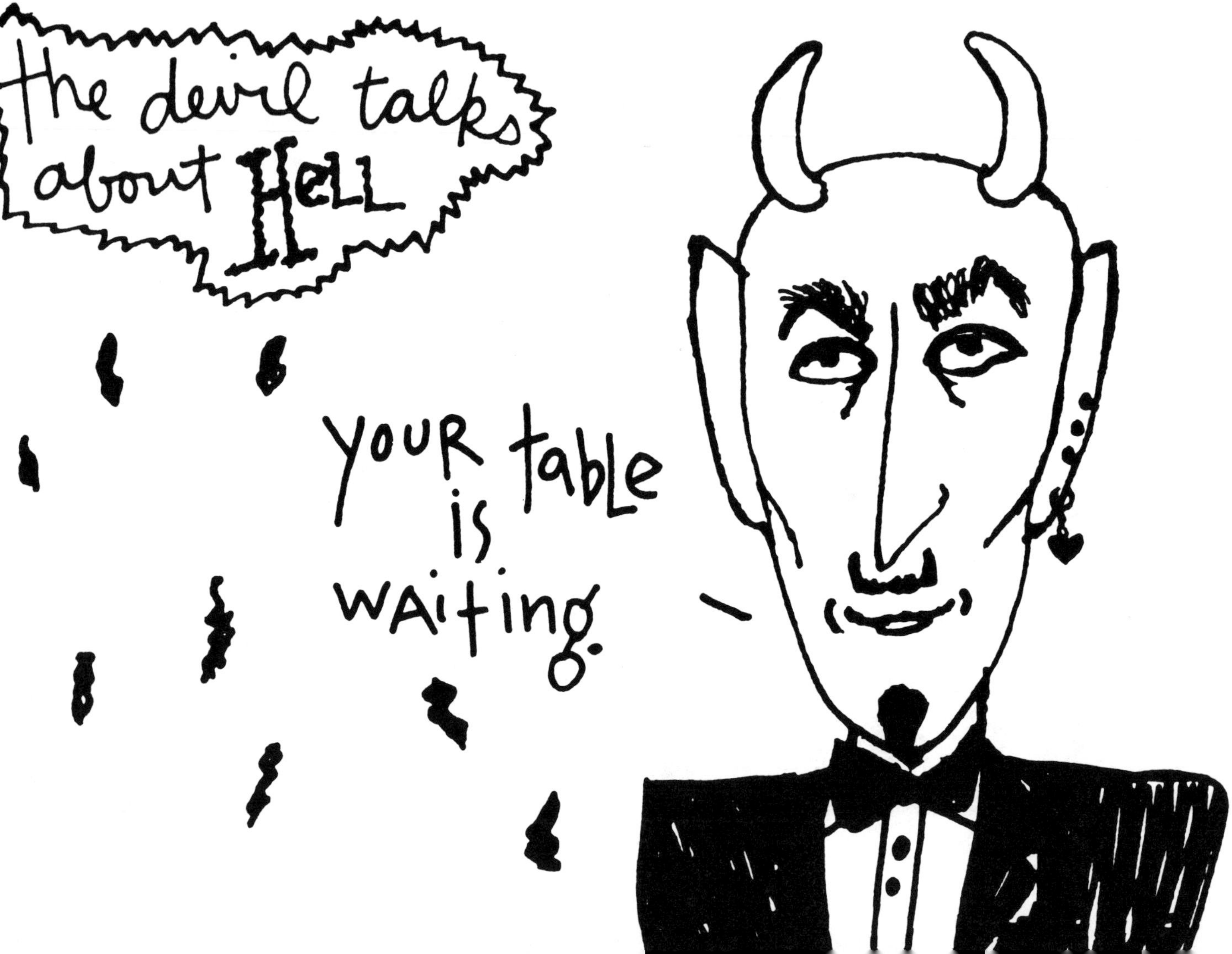
The devil talks about HELL
your table is waiting.

there is A special section in Hell for people who frequented French restaurants.

Let me get this STRAIGHT. IF I WANT ESCARGOT, I HAVE to CATCH the SNAILS AND DiP them IN GARLIC MYSELF?

oui.

the Way it Really happened: there are two sides to every story.

ADAM AND EVE

We were perfectly HAPPY IN EDEN. OUR LEAVING WAS the SNAKE'S FAULT. Totally.

the SNAKE DENIES RESPONSIBILITY

THEY CAME to ME. THEY SAID: "LISTEN, it's NICE HERE, BUT BORING. WE'D LIKE TO MOVE ON, BUT YOU KNOW HOW the BIG GUY IS.... HE WON'T LET US GO UNLESS HE thinks IT WAS HIS IDEA." I SAID: "LOOK, DO WHAT YOU WANT, BUT LEAVE ME OUT OF IT."

Ma! YOU SOUND terrible. OH, YOU READ THAT MAYONNAISE DOESN'T 'CAUSE "DEADLY TUNA FISH POISONING", IN FACT IT MAY ACTUALLY PROTECT FOOD FROM SPOILING.

YOU FEEL AS IF EVERYTHING YOU BELIEVE IN IS CRUMBLING. YOU DON'T EVEN KNOW IF YOU CAN TRUST the GOVERNMENT.

MA, SIT DOWN. I'VE GOT SOMETHING TO TELL YOU.

15

MA, WHEN ARE YOU COMING OUT?

Like some exotic plants, I FLOURISH where it's HUMID.

YOU'VE BEEN IN THERE FOUR HOURS.

MA, WHAT ARE YOU DOING IN THERE?

RITA, ARE YOU ON THE SUPREME COURT?

Lives of Susan

COMEDY MINI-SERIES ABOUT A WOMAN WHO HAS A 3-WAY SPLIT PERSONALITY: HOUSEWIFE, SNAKE HANDLER, AND EDUCATOR.

SUSAN LOOKS OUT THE WINDOW AND SEES HER NEIGHBOR WALKING HIS DOG ON HER LAWN. SHE PRESSES A BUTTON AND THE GROUND OPENS AND THE TWO OFFENDERS ARE WHISKED OFF TO AN UNDERGROUND RE-EDUCATION CENTER. LATER THEY ARE GIVEN A POOPER SCOOPER, A PLASTIC BAG, NEW IDENTITIES, AND RELEASED.

Little-Known Super-Heroes

Wonder Mom: Flying all over creation to see if she can make your life more pleasant.

Are you all right? You look a little peaked. Let me buy you dessert or a pair of Italian shoes. Give me the name of anyone who's hurt your feelings recently.

I'm fine. I'm not hungry. Who are you? Italian shoes? Sure.

DEATH ON TAP

I can't face another presidential campaign. I don't want to see any paid political announcements

There's a long way to go, kiddo. You better toughen up!

PRESIDENTIAL CAMPAIGN THERAPY

I don't want to hear about "bellwether" states. I don't want to hear the word "momentum."

I'm going to read you a partial list of presidential candidates. Don't whine.

the SUMMER is especially BUSY for *Love Cop*. MANY potentially INCOMPATIBLE couples meet At weddings OF MUTUAL FRIENDS. tHEY DRINK Lots OF CHAMPAGNE. Some OF them DANCE together, AND if the BAND is HALFWAY decent, they FALL IN Love.

WAit... it's oNLy the CHAMPAGNE AND the FRUit cocktAIL! FIND out HER credit RATiNG! He Likes JULIO IGLesIAs!

WAit JUSt A MiNUte!

Lives of Susan
comedy mini-series about a woman who has a 3-way split personality: housewife, maitre d' and landscape architect.

Susan is cleaning her flowers with a toothbrush when a group of her neighbors arrive to suggest that the 1,000 plastic daisies she planted in the front yard are an eyesore. Susan meekly removes them, but later covers the house and lawn with Belgian waffles.

Ma, what do you feed this plant?

Gatorade.

Ma, when are you coming out?

When they find out who really got the money that was diverted from the Iran arms deal.

What's that got to do with me? I haven't got it.

Easy to say. Hard to prove.

We sell no chips before their time.

PRICES PLUNGED SHARPLY TODAY...

NO BYE-BYE CELL-CELL BUT JAM JAM IN FUL MOON.

YOU DON'T HAVE A STOCK MARKET ON VENUS, SO ONCE A MONTH YOU PUT ON JACKETS,

ZZ.. BAll /NO /BIM! GREEN-BACKS.

GET TOGETHER IN A BIG ROOM AND HIT EACH OTHER WITH DOLLAR BILLS.

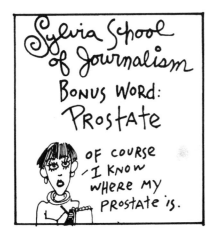

Sylvia School of Journalism

BONUS WORD: PROSTATE

OF COURSE I KNOW WHERE MY PROSTATE IS.

STUDENTS: PLEASE COMPLETE THE PARAGRAPH BELOW USING THE BONUS WORD PROSTATE ONCE MORE.

"YES," I SCREAMED, "IT'S TRUE. I ATE THE LAST COOKIE... I don't DESERVE TO LIVE," AND I THREW MYSELF PROSTATE BEFORE HIM.

How well do you know the Law?

Attorney General Meese lately expressed a desire to do away with the Miranda Law. What is the Miranda Law?

□ 1. Attorneys must appear in court wearing platform shoes and at least one piece of fruit in their hair.

□ 2. No, it's the accused who has to wear the banana.

the DEVIL trys to dissuade a potential client.

I'm willing to barter my soul to understand the new tax law.

I honestly don't think it's worth it.

Well, maybe I'd like to become a famous rock star and do outrageous things on stage.

Let's go with that one.

ILLEGAL USE OF GROWTH HORMONES IS ON THE RISE AMONG CATS.

DEAR CBS, LAST NIGHT I HAD AN EXCITING DREAM ABOUT A GAME SHOW THAT FEATURES THE RECENTLY DIVORCED. I THINK IT MIGHT BE JUST THE SHOT IN THE ARM YOUR NETWORK NEEDS.

FOR 10 POINTS, GLORIA, WHAT WILL YOUR EX-HUSBAND SAY IS YOUR MOST IRRITATING HABIT?

DAVE, WHO CARES?

EVERYTHING, DAVE.

test your Memory

"HASENFUS?" IT CERTAINLY SOUNDS FAMILIAR. I KNOW I KNOW THAT NAME. IS HE THAT INCREDIBLE YOUNG TENNIS PLAYER FROM WEST GERMANY?

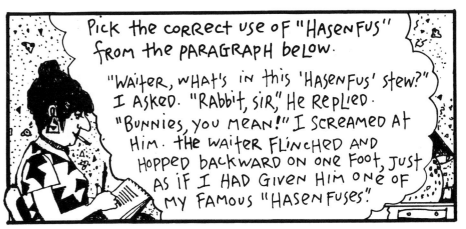

PICK THE CORRECT USE OF "HASENFUS" FROM THE PARAGRAPH BELOW.

"WAITER, WHAT'S IN THIS 'HASENFUS' STEW?" I ASKED. "RABBIT, SIR," HE REPLIED. "BUNNIES, YOU MEAN!" I SCREAMED AT HIM. THE WAITER FLINCHED AND HOPPED BACKWARD ON ONE FOOT, JUST AS IF I HAD GIVEN HIM ONE OF MY FAMOUS "HASENFUSES."

42

Lives of Susan – A comedy mini-series about a woman with multiple personalities: Brain surgeon, housewife and hair stylist.

Lives of Susan
Comedy mini-series about a woman with a 3-way split personality: Housewife, ethical relativist, and gourmet.

PASTE

While papering her husband's study in an intricate pattern of pit-bulls and golden retrievers, Susan puts her foot in the wallpaper paste for the third time. Her frustration makes her ravenous, and she eats a copy of "the Frugal Gourmet."

How well do you know your clichés?

He's driving me crazy.

Men, you can't live with 'em and... I forgot the rest.

Please complete: "Men/women, you can't live with 'em and you can't..

☐ 1. Dip them in batter for tempura."
☐ 2. Use them for collateral on a loan."
☐ 3. Put in new batteries."

ALIENS TAKE OVER A MC DONALD'S

HOW WELL DO YOU KNOW YOUR NEIGHBORHOOD?

YOU DESPERATELY WANT TO SLEEP IN ON A SUNDAY. WHAT WILL WAKE YOU UP AT 6:30 A.M.?

☐ 1. AN OLD MAN STANDING BELOW YOUR WINDOW COUGHING AND SPITTING REPEATEDLY.

☐ 2. A CAR ALARM.

☐ 3. YOUR CATS STARING AT YOU FROM ON TOP OF YOUR CHEST.

HI, MOM. WHAT'S UP? YOU HAD A DREAM ABOUT ME? A NICE DREAM, I HOPE.

YOU DREAMT THAT ALL THE CONTAMINATED DRUGS THAT WERE PULLED OFF STORE SHELVES ENDED UP IN MY MEDICINE CHEST?

YOU WANT ME TO CHECK MY MEDICINE CHEST RIGHT NOW?

TODAY the STOCK MARKET PLUNGED AND THEN ROSE SHARPLY INJURING SEVERAL HUNDRED PEOPLE.

Interfering Super Cops - policing the COUNTRY MAKING SURE YOU BUY WHAT everyone else is BUYING.

SUPER COP BERATES A COUPLE IN THEIR KITCHEN.

WHAT DO YOU MEAN YOU DON'T HAVE A MICROWAVE OVEN? AREN'T YOU EMBARRASSED IN FRONT OF YOUR FRIENDS? THAT IS, IF YOU HAVE ANY FRIENDS, WHICH I DOUBT.

TELL HER WE'LL GET ONE VERY SOON.

SHE'S HERE AGAIN.

Alien Love: CAN A WOMAN FROM A LARGE MIDWESTERN TOWN FIND LOVE AND UNDERSTANDING ON A FAR DISTANT PLANET?

ON THANKSGIVING WE HAVE ROAST TURKEY WITH 2 KINDS OF STUFFING, GRAVY, SWEET POTATOES, PUMPKIN PIE WITH WHIPPED CREAM

SOUNDS DELICIOUS.

"AND DO YOU INVITE LESS FORTUNATE PEOPLE TO SHARE THIS MARVELOUS THANKSGIVING DINNER WITH YOU?" HE ASKED SMILING HAPPILY. "OH, OF COURSE WE DO," I SAID, BLUSHING, STAMMERING AND IN GENERAL LYING THROUGH MY TEETH.

SYLVIA SCHOOL OF HISTORICAL WRITING BONUS VOCABULARY WORD: "CAMISOLE"

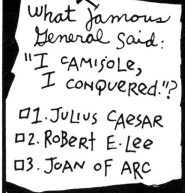

What famous General Said: "I CAMISOLE, I CONQUERED."?

☐ 1. JULIUS CAESAR
☐ 2. ROBERT E. LEE
☐ 3. JOAN OF ARC

PLEASE COMPLETE THIS PARAGRAPH USING THE WORD "CAMISOLE" ONE MORE TIME:

"DARLIN', PLEASE FETCH ME MY CAMISOLE, THIS SUN'S ABOUT TO FRECKLE ME TO A CRISP," MOANED SCARLETT.

The Sylvia School of Horror Story Writing

-There's something in the basement.

Let's introduce it to the thing in the attic.

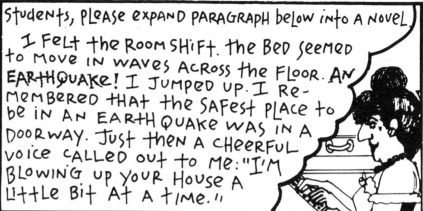

Students, please expand paragraph below into a novel.

I felt the room shift. The bed seemed to move in waves across the floor. An EARTHQUAKE! I jumped up. I remembered that the safest place to be in an earthquake was in a doorway. Just then a cheerful voice called out to me: "I'M BLOWING UP YOUR HOUSE A LITTLE BIT AT A TIME."

I'm never going to say an unkind word about Ralph again. I make him sound like a monster, and really he's a wonderful person.

I've always liked Ralph.

That's because you don't know his ways like I do.

The man is dirt. If he were a car, he'd be recalled.

An open Letter to Hollywood Executives. Gentlemen: Now, I don't like teen-agers any more than the next person, but

Do you REALLY THINK we Need ANY MORE MOVIES WHERE they Get MURDERED by A MANIAC EVERY-time they Get toGETHER IN A GROUP? Love Syl.

DOGS FROM HELL

the Dogs from Hell pretend to be cats to Lure gullible Burglars.

meow, meow

-meow. purr purr.

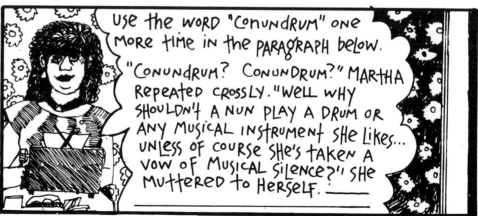

AND NOW AN Editorial Reply from Ms. S. Lake, president of G.R.I.T. (GALs Reform Income tAx) suggesting AN Alternative proposal For tAX Reform Reflecting the present inequality of MEN'S AND WOMEN'S WAGES.

the Devil sugar-coats the pill
I can't stand the suspense. How will I die?
At the opera. You'll fall asleep during the first act as usual, only this time you don't wake up.

No. that's totally unacceptable. I'm willing to sell my soul for a more glorious, end.

Okay. You parachute into a tiny country ruled by a cruel despot. You make your way to the palace and assassinate him. A grateful populace carries you on their shoulders to the opera and <u>then</u> you kick off.

REMEMBER: "YOU CAN'T TAKE IT WITH YOU."

SO EAT IT NOW.

SURVEY QUESTION OF THOSE PEOPLE ON A WIDE-BODY PLANE WHOSE HANDS ARE WELDED TO THEIR ARM RESTS, AND WHOSE SKIN IS CLAMMY TO THE TOUCH.

WHAT DO YOU HOPE NEVER TO HEAR YOUR PILOT SAY?

☐1. "HI, THIS IS YOUR PILOT. I HAD THE WORST FIGHT OF MY LIFE WITH MY WIFE THIS MORNING."

☐2. "LET'S SEE HOW FAST THIS BABY WILL GO."

☐3. "WHOOPS."

65

MR. FAUBUS OF "NMEN" (NO MORE ELITIST NONSENSE) IS HERE TO REBUT OUR EDITORIAL LAMENTING THE LOW STANDARDS SHOWN IN REAGAN'S RECENT JUDICIAL APPOINTMENTS.

I'M SICK OF ALL THIS TALK ABOUT CHOOSING ONLY THE "BEST" FOR FEDERAL JUDGESHIPS. IS THIS A DEMOCRACY OR WHAT? WE WANT AVERAGE GUYS ON THE BENCH, SAME GOES FOR SURGEONS.

CONSTANT NOSE-BLOWING CAN AGGRAVATE OR ACTUALLY CAUSE RESPIRATORY INFECTIONS WHEREAS SNIFFLING...

CAN CAUSE MURDER.

IF I GIVE UP MY CAREER AND STAY HOME WITH MY KIDS I'M AFRAID I'LL REGRET it. IF I HAVE KIDS AND keep working, I'LL FEEL GUILTY. IF I DON'T HAVE KIDS I'LL REGRET it... HELP!

YOU WILL SLEEP NOW, AND WHEN YOU WAKE YOU WILL HAVE ONLY ONE REGRET...

SYLVIA'S HEALING HYPNOSIS.

Lives of Susan

A comedy mini-series about a woman with a 3-way split personality: housewife, plastic surgeon and Charles Bronson look-alike.

Susan is drinking coffee and looking out into the backyard when she notices that her herb garden is overrun by crabgrass. Her fury brings out her Charles Bronson persona and she attacks the offensive weeds with a semi-automatic weapon, decimating the crabgrass, a 2-car garage and a weber grill.

A Pepsi and an orange pop... no, make it two Pepsis.

Insulting Superheroes

5-3

the Real Estate Cop visits a Wimpy Couple

You rent this apartment? Rent?! Don't you know that owning your own home is part of the American dream? You disgust me.

Tell her we have a friend who's in real estate.

She's here — again.

73

Alien Love—the continuing story of love on a far distant planet.

It's Valentine's Day—I ♥ have a surprise for you.

I tried to look PLEASED, but I remembered the time he brought Liberace and the Smothers Brothers to serenade me, and I screamed: "What is it this time?!" "Look", he said, pointing outside where the entire planetary fleet was flying in a heart-shaped formation. "Wow!" I said feeling ashamed of my earlier outburst, and I was about to apologize when I saw the piano and candelabra.

Results of survey question asked of people standing in front of a candy display who had recently given up smoking.

WHAT REMARKS DO YOU HATE TO HEAR THE MOST?

1. "Now that you quit smoking, you'll eat like a horse."

2. "When I quit, I got cranky and irritable, luckily in your case no one will notice."

Lives of Susan

COMEDY MINI-SERIES ABOUT A WOMAN WHO HAS A 3-WAY SPLIT PERSONALITY: HOUSEWIFE, PERIODONTIST, AND PARAPSYCHOLOGIST.

SUSAN DREAMS THAT HER HUSBAND TURNS INTO A SEVEN-FOOT IGUANA WHO CONFESSES TO BEING A CIA AGENT. "I DON'T REALLY WORK DOWNTOWN," HE SAID. "I'VE BEEN FLYING SECRET MISSIONS TO CENTRAL AMERICA." "WELL," SAID SUSAN, "NO ONE CAN HELP TURNING INTO A GIANT REPTILE, BUT A CIA AGENT—THAT'S REALLY WEIRD."

Be Prepared for some surprises at the pearly gates.
HAVE YOUR I.D.'s READY.

81

Sylvia School of Writing

BONUS WORD: "QUANDARY"

Pick the sentence in which "QUANDARY" is used correctly.

☐1. "He looked around and saw that he was in some sort of abandoned QUANDARY. In the distance he heard a motor starting up... My God! It was a huge earthmoving machine—they were going to leave him in this QUANDARY, under a ton of LANDFILL."

☐2. "He was in a huge empty QUANDARY. The washing machines were silent now, but someone was sitting at the MANGLE... someone who had NO FACE!"

MAN GOES BANANAS.

The DEVIL TALKS ABOUT HELL

HELL is not the same all the time.

THIS MONTH IN HELL: YOU HAVE TO WATCH A VIDEO OF YOURSELF...

ON YOUR FIRST DATE—OVER AND OVER.

the WAY it REALLY HAPPENED: the SNAKE TALKS EVE INTO ASKING GOD FOR A COMPANION, AND HE CREATES ADAM.

ADAM'S FIRST DAY

this PLACE'S A MESS.

YOUR PERFUME'S A BIT STRONG ISN'T IT? HAVE YOU SEEN MY SOCKS? COULD YOU SPEAK IN COMPLETE SENTENCES?

YO! GOD! I THINK I MADE A MISTAKE.

CAT MANIPULATIONS.

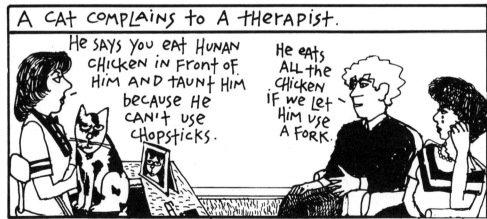

A CAT COMPLAINS TO A THERAPIST.

He SAYS YOU EAT HUNAN CHICKEN IN FRONT OF HIM AND TAUNT HIM BECAUSE HE CAN'T USE CHOPSTICKS.

He EATS ALL THE CHICKEN IF WE LET HIM USE A FORK.

GAME SHOWS OF the future

HAS some-one been SHRINKING YOUR CLOTHES?

Dear Syl, after 30 years the thrill of seeing the seasons change has paled, and I'm planning to move to a warmer climate. I'm worried that my friends won't understand. What do you think?

Sign me—"FED-UP IN THE WINDY CITY."

87

Animals use their clout in Heaven.

Did you ever laugh out loud when your pet tried to jump up on the couch and missed?

A tiny smile may have played across my lips, but nothing more.

Menacing super cops of the future.

The Exercise Cop, acting on a tip from someone you thought was a friend, pays you an evening visit.

Show me your health club membership card now! Do you have a program of regular exercise? How often do you run? Where is your stationary bike? Stand up when I talk to you!

SYLVIA'S mini action film quiz.

Pick the correct title of ARNOLD SCHWARZENEGGER'S newest ACTION FLICK.

☐1. PROCRASTINATOR
☐2. PREDATOR
☐3. JANITOR

WHAT is the NAME OF SYLVESTER STALLONE'S newest RELEASE?

☐1. HYENA
☐2. COBRA
☐3. CANDELABRA.

RING

RING RING

Hi. You HAVE REACHED "DIAL-A-REST." CAN'T SLEEP? WORRIED ABOUT NUCLEAR ACCIDENTS? START HUMMING (to the TUNE OF "I CAN'T GET NO SATISFACTION"): ♪♪ "I CAN'T GET NO RADIATION, NO, NO NO." ♪ Now TAKE A DEEP BREATH, HOLD IT... LET IT OUT THROUGH YOUR MOUTH, BANG YOUR HEAD AGAINST THE WALL. REST, AND REPEAT.

LADIES AND GENTLEMEN, this is YOUR CAPTAIN. WE'RE GOING to EXECUTE A MANEUVER CALLED A "POWER BACK" IN WHICH WE BACK RAPIDLY AWAY FROM the GATE, DO A BACK FLIP AND LAND ON tHAT LITTLE CESSNA to YOUR RIGHT. PLEASE EXTINGUISH ALL SMOKING MATERIALS.

the Sylvia School of Dental Writing. Bonus Words:

TARTAR
AND
PLAQUE.

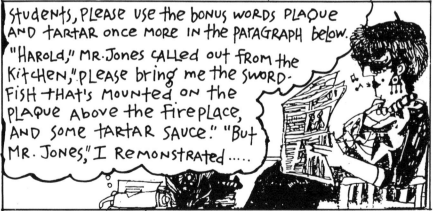

STUDENTS, PLEASE USE the BONUS WORDS PLAQUE AND TARTAR ONCE MORE IN the PARAGRAPH BELOW.

"HAROLD," MR. JONES CALLED OUT FROM the KITCHEN, "PLEASE bring ME the SWORD-FISH tHAT'S MOUNTED ON the PLAQUE ABOVE the FIREPLACE, AND SOME TARTAR SAUCE." "BUT MR. JONES," I REMONSTRATED.....

I'M ELOPING ON FRIDAY.

the **Nutrition Cop**, ACTING ON A TIP, PAYS AN EARLY MORNING VISIT TO A LITTLE GIRL.

I HEAR YOU AND YOUR MOM ARE going OUT FOR BREAKFAST.

UH HUH! WE'RE GOIN' TO DUNKIN' DONUTS.

OH NO! DON'T TELL HER.

Hi. Are you normally a right-winger but you woke up this morning thinking: "there should be more women in Congress," or "I must write a check to MEDICAL AID FOR EL SALVADOR?" You may be the victim of "PROGRESSIVE MIND CONTROL". Leave your name and number and we'll get back to you with our exorcism schedule.

T.V. Nostalgia Quiz

This is a trompe l'oeil fridge

Famous for his large ears and devastating logic, this beloved television character's name is..?

☐1. Dr. Spock
☐2. Mr. Spock
☐3. Howdy Doody.

I never —"Miss the Kitty Litter." She keeps moving it AROUND— FOR WHAT REASON I CAN'T GUESS.

...the ARticle CONCLudeS tHAt woMEN oveR 40 HAve StAt'StiCALly 'AS MuCH CHANCE of getting MARRied AS of getting KILLeD By A terROR'st.

WHAt ARe the odds that they MARRY A terRORiSt?

Sylvia's School
of Writing
for Magazines

Aspiring Journalists,
complete the
following
sentence from
the choices
below.

there MAY be some tempting LEFtovers inside....

OR A couple OF ANGRY DOBERMANS...

DEPENDS ON YOUR KARMA.

Sylvia's Tales from the Crypt

this week JASON RETURNS to the HOUSE ON ELM ST. ACROSS FROM the CEMETERY WHERE they spit oN YOUR GRAVE.

LioneL awoke suddeNly. He was AFRaid. Outside, somewHERE iN the distaNce He HEARD A discreet cougH. He FoRced His trembling HaNDs to open the dresser dRawer WHERE the LozeNges WERE kept. He couLd oNLy PRay they'd be satisfied with Sucrets.....FOR they were the VampiRES WHO COUGH iN the NiGHt.

today in Hollywood, A spokesman for the movie industry announced that they would no longer make movies aimed at the teen-age market.

112

'Love Cop': RUSHING AROUND HITHER AND YON TRYING TO PREVENT INCOMPATIBLE PEOPLE FROM BECOMING INVOLVED.

WAIT! DON'T TELL EACH OTHER YOUR LAST NAMES.

YOU THINK GORBACHEV WRECKED THE SUMMIT, AND I THINK IT WAS THAT IDIOT REAGAN, YET... I'M DRAWN IRRESISTIBLY TO YOU.

I THINK YOU'RE ONE STEP AWAY FROM BEING A COMMIE, BUT YOUR HAIR... THOSE EYES...

FIRE! PLEASE EVACUATE THE PREMISES. YOU'LL THANK ME LATER.

HI MOM. YOU WANT ME TO PROMISE NOT TO EAT ANY FOOD IN A RESTAURANT SERVED ON CHIPPED CROCKERY,

BECAUSE DANGEROUS GERMS CAN LODGE IN THE CHIPS? SO IT'S OKAY IF I EAT SUSHI AS LONG AS IT'S SERVED ON AN UNCHIPPED PLATE?

MOM, I SWEAR I WAS ONLY TEASING. I WOULD NEVER EAT ANYTHING COOKED FOR LESS THAN 30 MINUTES.

SYLVIA'S "BRING BACK THOSE GOOD OLD WORDS NOBODY USES ANY MORE" SCHOOL OF WRITING.

Bonus Phrase: "RESTRICTIVE COVENANT"

PICK THE CORRECT DEFINITION OF "RESTRICTIVE COVENANT" FROM THE CHOICES BELOW.

☐ 1. LONG, NARROW OVERALL SUPPOSEDLY FAVORED BY 19th CENTURY WITCHES.

☐ 2. KINKY SEXUAL PRACTICE PREVALENT IN THE 40's AND 50's.

IF YOU KEEP DOING THAT, YOUR EYES WILL STAY THAT WAY.

Ring, Ring,

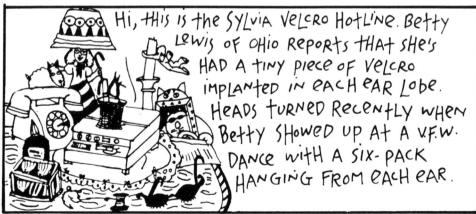

Hi, THIS IS THE SYLVIA VELCRO HOTLINE. BETTY LEWIS OF OHIO REPORTS THAT SHE'S HAD A TINY PIECE OF VELCRO IMPLANTED IN EACH EAR LOBE. HEADS TURNED RECENTLY WHEN BETTY SHOWED UP AT A V.F.W. DANCE WITH A SIX-PACK HANGING FROM EACH EAR.

I DREAMT THAT I REPLACED VANNA WHITE ON THE "WHEEL OF FORTUNE", BUT WHEN I REFUSED TO WEAR HER OLD DRESSES, PAT SAJAK AND RICHARD DAWSON STRAPPED ME TO THE "WHEEL" AND I WON A BILLIARD TABLE AND A TRIP TO BERMUDA.

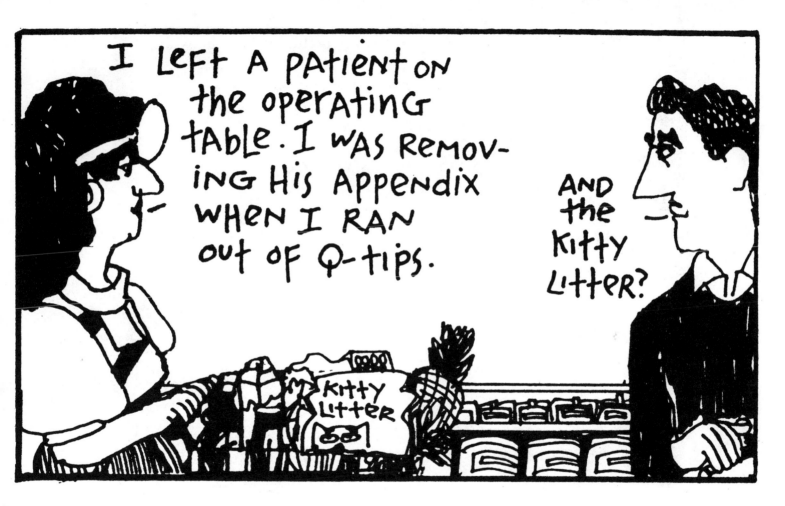

CAT LIES of the RICH AND FAMOUS.

JUST BECAUSE there's GOOSE DOWN ALL OVER YOUR BEDROOM DOESN'T MEAN THAT SOME-ONE ACCIDENTALLY RIPPED A HOLE IN YOUR COMFORTER. MAYBE SOME GEESE GOT INTO YOUR BOUDOIR.

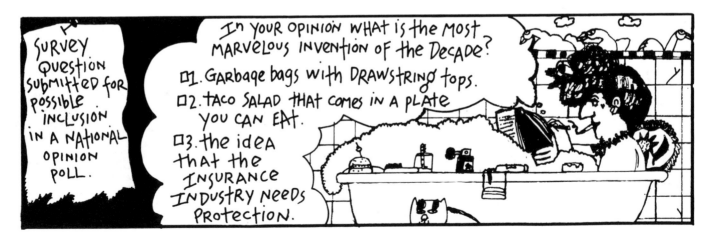

SURVEY QUESTION SUBMITTED FOR POSSIBLE INCLUSION IN A NATIONAL OPINION POLL.

IN YOUR OPINION WHAT IS THE MOST MARVELOUS INVENTION OF THE DECADE?

☐1. GARBAGE BAGS WITH DRAWSTRING tops.

☐2. TACO SALAD THAT COMES IN A PLATE YOU CAN EAT.

☐3. the IDEA THAT the INSURANCE INDUSTRY NEEDS PROTECTION.

HARRY, IF YOU EAT SOMETHING WITH YOUR EYES CLOSED, IT TASTES COMPLETELY DIFFERENT. ARE YOUR EYES CLOSED? Good.

OKAY, REACH DOWN AND TAKE A BITE OUTTA THAT CHEESEBURGER I JUST PUT IN FRONT OF YOU. GOOD. HOW DOES IT TASTE?

UGH! IT DOESN'T EVEN TASTE LIKE MEAT.

IT'S CRISCO ON A SESAME SEED BUN.

SO IT IS.

STAY TUNED FOR "STRIP THE GUEST" THE SUNDAY MORNING NEWS SHOW WHERE REPORTERS ASK THE HARD QUESTIONS, AND POLITICIANS HAVE TO REMOVE AN ARTICLE OF CLOTHING FOR EACH EVASIVE ANSWER.

CATS CAN'T
take the
FIFTH
AMENDMENT.

ABOUT THE AUTHOR

Nicole Hollander lives quietly in Chicago with her two cats and a small flock of Shetland ponies.